EXPLORING IDENTITY

EXPLORING IDENTITY

LUNA EMBER

CONTENTS

CHAPTER 1

Introduction

This book explores our fascination with femininity and how it is related to identity on the individual, cultural, and social level. I focus here on two sets of stories about identity and femininity – one about cross-dressing, the other about men who have undergone gender reassignment surgery but are now contemplating or have actually returned to living as men. Both sets of stories have attracted significant media attention, suggesting that these are topics of some interest, and debate on websites suggests they are also met with a range of responses from those upholding cis-privilege. Conversations – more or less public – about these topics, both in the academic and non-academic arena, are filled with assumptions about why men might want to get in touch with their 'feminine side' (cross-dressers) or live as women (transsexuals).

Having drawn attention to these different frames for thinking about the behavior depicted in these stories, we wish here to draw purer attention to the description of the behavior itself and to document it further with reference to interviews with white, UK-London-based, cross-dressers who self-define themselves as different 'types' of person or who have drawn more intriguing social theories from their dress. This descriptive project and the apposite reflections upon the material have value in themselves as one means of bringing the topic of identity in closer. We might argue that the cross-dressing case itself begins to complicate dualistic thinking since it reveals performance and being as intimately linked rather than the latter as prior and fundamental; as one cross-dresser asks caustically 'What do people do it for – second nature?' (see also Garfinkel 1967).

CHAPTER 2

Historical Perspectives on Crossdressing

Throughout history, crossdressing has been practiced in some form in virtually every human culture. Crossdressing behavior of cross-dressed individuals is replete in ancient mythology and is even discussed by Hippocrates in his treatise "The Nature of Women". The practice of women performing men's roles spanned diverse historical periods and societies, including the Iroquois of upland New York, the Nez Perce of the Pacific Northwest, the indigenous societies of Africa, the Pacific Islands, Melanesian kava societies, rural communities in Bohemia, New Spain, and the Inuit of the Y-k Delta in Alaska. With regard to the public performances of men in women's clothing, there is some evidence for this during the Middle Ages in Europe. Despite varying social attitudes and governmental policies directed against it, crossdressing became a visible feature of American society during the 19th century, finding expression in both popular culture and in the lived experience of individuals who will remain relatively invisible and largely undocumented by history. An entire sub-genre of nineteenth- and early twentieth-century dime novels focuses on women who take to the high seas as men to save their fathers, freedom, or loves.

Societal attitudes towards men who dressed or personated spirits gradually became transformed in Western Europe. The newly popular notion that many of those practicing crossdressing were simply "women confined to men's clothing" often led to society treating the individuals more leniently. In time, legal attitudes which had targeted specific forms of women's "disguise" declined both in England and America. Consequently, by the start of the 18th century, one could say that there existed a pre-20th-century equivalent of "Don't Ask, Don't Tell" regarding the topic of crossdressing and transgender issues in English law and society. As crossdressing history moved into the 20th century, a newly forming medical establishment strove valiantly to dismiss powers previously held by traditional priesthoods and to begin its own investigation of gender motives, identities, and etiologies. Establishment definitions of crossdressing have largely framed the popular imagination of crossdressing still prevalent today.

CHAPTER 3

Psychological and Societal Implications of Crossdr

Crossdressing does not raise any moral questions about possessive identity or ontology as some essentialist transgender theories do. While crossdressing theory in the United States is quite limited, crossdressing has begun to garner attention from the medical and psychological community in Canada, Australia and the United Kingdom. It is not transvestism that is the problem but trans-vestiture, the transformation of the private, secret body through the clothes into the socially approved, decent one. The problem of crossdressing is not political, it is psychological. The removal of a simple legal barrier is necessary but by no means sufficient to one's mental health.

The act of crossdressing is at the very least to violate social norms whereby the male is assigned certain apparel and has already been attributed a gender-appropriate, non-transvestite self. The reason for the social embarrassment concerning crossdressing has more to do with psychology than social ensnarement or politics. After all, crossdressing is not illegal in most Western democracies, with the exception of a few states here in the United States. You can go in public, grocery shopping, bar-hopping and cinema-going all over the United States crossdressed with neither law enforcement nor Gestapo-like retributions.

CHAPTER 4

Gender Identity and Expression

What is the relationship between crossdressing and gender identity? It seems that crossdressing, while it can be used to explore gender roles and presentation, also indicates a cognizance—conscious or otherwise—of one's gender beyond the crossdressed state. I raise this point because in my own practice, and in the narratives presented by many of the "members" of the Fictionmania community, crossdressing seems to be a means of gender expression rather than a solid statement on gender identity.

Gender presentation is distinct from gender identity. This presents interesting complexities when trying to achieve a coherent theory of gender which accounts for the complex bits like mannerisms, personality traits, and clothing that seem to be keyed to gender but which are not part of the "meat" of gender. It also smudges the edges of a theory of "failed" presentations: to what extent can someone attempt (and fail) to present their gender in a way that is culturally legible? In my case, I often express my gender identity through clothing that I find comfortable, ignore gestures of gender presentation such as makeup, hair accessories, and jewelry, and show my body hair—this is treated as a woman's "right," the right to be edgy. In my case, expressing myself as a woman with an edgy gender shows that I am trans. "This is my man and I'm sticking with him!" I do not have an active gender identity to be treated in such a manner, and thus my expression is not recognized by such a public. This public is therefore presented with a non-woman, no matter what impression might be left by my presentation—only those who can see the wholeness of the universe and the hidden depths of my soul can be said to see me as "truly" female. Less solipsistically, the experience of trying to convince people that one is one gender with one's body while appearing to be another is just living as a transgender person; it is not particular to transitioning, per se.

CHAPTER 5

Crossdressing in Popular Culture

Crossdressing as a practice has a long history in human cultures. It is often thought of as deviant behavior, however, how media and culture have portrayed crossdressing has greatly affected how the public perceives the practice.

As far back as the Renaissance, crossdressing has figured in Western theater. Through the centuries, in venues ranging from Shakespeare's Globe Theater to Paris's Moulin Rouge, crossdressing—or, as it is often called in the theater, "dressing in drag"—has seeped into popular culture. This entertainment practice has spurred such popularity that an entire gay subculture has developed from it. Crossdressers have become celebrities in various fields—everyone from John Wayne to Andre the Giant has donned a dress, in their roles as "members" of the opposite sex. And in restaurants in Paris, "transvestite ballets" have inspired such creative works as Gay Paris, Victor Herbert's North African opera. Victor Herbert later created the operetta Naughty Marietta just so people would see the showgirls he had hired donning Spanish costumes. A number of movie favorites have also used male crossdresser heroines, including classic films such as Billy Wilder's Some Like It Hot, with Tony Curtis and Jack Lemmon crossdressing to get into an all-girl swing band.

Within the last four decades, crossdressing has become a specialty subculture, born of the convergence of several cultural movements. Drag shows have become popular in young urban centers, and participation in ball culture is now increasingly percolating through rap as young straight people are influenced by Queer Nation. David Bowie, a bisexual musician, was well-known for his place among teenagers as a glam-rock superstar who attracted the rising minority of teens who are not heterosexual and their friends. Even punk rock partook of this movement, playing directly with gender roles in such acts as Jayne County. The popularity of such acts as Sylvia Rivera speaks to the interest that urbanites have in exploring crossdressing as a space wherein the norms of heterosexuality and the body are subverted. The Carnival ball in Rio de Janeiro includes a value shift where the king becomes a peasant and men wear dresses; Halloween in the same vein features teenagers in not their own gender roles. Many people costume in the other sex role daily, but those who are not transgendered typically spend a great deal of energy in denying that they are doing it for erotic reasons.

CHAPTER 6

Crossdressing and Male Feminization in Literature

Though literature is not the focus of this article, cross-dressing and male feminization appear frequently among the topics and themes in the writing of newer performance artists. Indeed, more and more scholarly interventions on image making and subjugated subjectivity introduce discussion of contemporary performance. Here we might think of John Harrington's thesis on claimsmakers (2005) or Marjorie N. Feld's examination of the historical roots of sympathy in popular music (2008). Yet cross-dressing and male feminization have also appeared as comedic or even negative themes in the pages of Dignity. In the same issue as our next essay, Ron Jacobs derides the gender hybridity of contemporary feminists in "Put Down that Sledgehammer" (The Chronicler, 2(3)). He follows the work of Seyward Goodhand, who in a public letter to be found below, cautions women's studies scholars not to dilute their political movement by "subsuming feminism under some larger, looser, non-threatening, trans-movement." On campus, we can often find flyers for drag shows that blithely promote "tits and cocktails" or showcase a pouting, young boy posing in high heels. In mainstream literature, contemporary works by the likes of Ian McEwan, Martin Amis, and Douglas Coupland have featured male characters presented in feminine roles or cross-dressing scenarios. The practice of boys dressing as girls is also rendered as a comedic "theme" in the Hollywood movie Big Momma's House, however, I am unable to comment on how faithful the film is to boys' lives, the practice of cross-dressing, or to male feminization. In traditional literature, depictions of male characters engaging in cross-dressing and male feminization may be given a tertiary treatment, including storylines emphasizing individuals' transitions from men to women. The book Madame Doubtfire (later made into a feature film) depicts a male character, dismayed at the family's decision to hire an out-of-work actor, dressing as a nanny to infiltrate the household, and is used by Davies to report in brief on a transsexual boy who had undergone surgery.

The effect of the above representations is the offering up of boys dressed as girls as somehow an interesting pique into humanity, or a living action for a better understanding of cross-dressing's lust, love, and sexual orientation. Both the genre and description of cross-dressing further hand over the bodies of cross-dressed males to the whims of theological/historical theorist, medical practitioner, and social psychologist. For most, the very idea of a boy in girl's clothing exists in a novel, punctuated dimension that generally extends no further than to exemplify or complicate an argument. Whether literature is art or artifice, it is the manner in which the fictional word is approached and hypostatized as experience that most interests me and, ultimately, any reader of such worlds. In the following essay, cross-dressing and male feminization operate as more than clinical or documentary fodder and, whether authors of fiction are ennui-centric or homophobic misogynists, they set up a discordant point along an expansive, surrounding universe. Deeply rooted in narrative experience and the locus of a boy in female garb, Harriet Wadeson hands over a short story written by D.J. Levin to a treatment not dissimilar to that of a process diary or case study. Harriet Wadeson writes that it is not clear whether the story is written by a cross-dresser seeking therapy, a compassionate therapist seeking treatment for his cross-dresser patient, or neither. This maximally anti-encompassing position encourages multiple responses to seeing cross-dressing. For instance, the potential encounter with a non-cis body moving through the clinic may bring our theoretical, or "theoretical," point systems – our decades-deep queers, our newly-minted neuroqueerists – into stark, irreconcilable relief against the body trembled beneath Harriet Wadeson's fingers.

CHAPTER 7

Intersectionality: Race, Class, and Crossdressing

All of our identities are complex. In Canada, one of the most common ways that we define people is by the physical markers of race, phenotype, ethnicity, and religion. We also define people by their sexual orientation and gender. Such things are used to judge people as an automatic function of most people's encounters and create large-scale and private discrimination. Everyone is often much more than just their identity. As an economic system strives to define us all similarly (e.g. as workers, owners, poor, rich, and so on), it frequently makes it extremely distressing to handle the pressure of racism, the wounds of genocidal dispossession, and the emotional stress of xenophobia or transphobia. Amponsa and Boyle argue that all of these circumstances reaffirm the power of capital, and the way that we determine who is allowed to be and define themselves as a woman is connected to the struggles over rates of wages.

Clearly, it is necessary to understand that people of all sorts can crossdress and that male feminization can occur in the cisgendered and heterosexual populations. Interruptions of interpersonal interactions, mental health, and violence are the constant threats to margin heteropatriarchy: the way that we punish people for their gender expression is not contingent on binary definitions of gender; it is contingent on the capacity of a community to predicate value and violence on individuals. Thus, the ability to crossdress is reserved for the well-off and for the white in intersection with class. Furthermore, race often makes certain acts of crossdressing or male feminization nearly impossible.

CHAPTER 8

Crossdressing and LGBTQ+ Communities

Crossdressing shares a long history and has a great deal of overlap with other members of the LGBTQ+ communities. Even crossdressers who do not pursue or have phalloplasties encounter many of the same issues as those who do, including the extent of personal identity alignment with social or political views of crossdressing, normativity and categorization, bodily and necessary medical practices, and the contingencies of stereotype and self-stigma. Despite the overlap, each of these identity groups also experiences unique social issues, particularly in terms of socially prescribed body norms and subjectivities.

Some members of the transgender communities find themselves having to defend their womanhood in the face of systematic oppression, including structural constraints on their access to PDOs and breast surgery as well as institutional practices related to gender designations and markers. Many men seeking PDOs, or orchiectomies (surgical removal of the testicles), also face institutional constraints on their access to medical providers who will perform the surgeries they seek. These men are likely to be required to prostitute themselves, sell drugs or sex, or present in such a way as to fit the psychiatric diagnostic category of Gender Identity Disorder or trans-sexualism. In short, there is a network of intersecting regulations and practices that monitor the lives of male-bodied people who do not meet dominant visual and physical stereotypes in ways that reduce opportunities for confronting body concerns openly, outwardly, and publicly. Sex reassignment, sexual affiliation, and the ability to expose non-normative gender are differently loaded for each group.

CHAPTER 9

Crossdressing and Mental Health

There are currently nine publications addressing crossdressing and its impact on mental health. It is important to investigate the nature of crossgender identity as it relates to overall mental health. The stigma often associated with male feminization, whether considered for homosexual orientation, pre-androgen replacement desires, autogynephilia, or other concerns, could place cross-gender people at higher risk for mental health concerns. This brief literature review looks at crossdressing from the perspective of the well-being of the practitioner, or what has been referred to as the autogynephilic type.

Crossdressing has been seen as a part of fetish and compulsive disorders. Many authors and clinicians consider the underlying causes of these disorders to be emotional distress, psychological trauma, or mental health issues. However, in recent years, authors have begun to argue that the compulsive behavior associated can be separated from the mental health issues. Some papers argued individuals can be freely fetishistic towards the activities of crossdressing, engaging without gender identity issues. Others have also framed male feminization as a type of resistance and non-conforming behavior; individuals must regulate this behavior for emotional health. Gender identity diagnosis is one of the few "mental/physical diseases" from which individuals can request and often receive treatment. Mental health providers need to be aware of the national guidelines that outline care for individuals requiring sex reassignment support.

CHAPTER 10

Crossdressing and Body Image

Crossdressing has been anecdotally reported by some in the transgender literature to have a beneficial effect on the crossdresser's own body image, even though no evidence supports the claim. This study, involving 100 participants, is the first we are aware of to directly assess the influence of crossdressing – and the manner by which best androgynous appearance can be achieved/accessed – on body image. We asked participants to indicate their feelings towards their appearance when adopting a typically male, typically female, or androgynous style, and when looking in a mirror during each of the three dressing conditions. We found that when crossdressed, participants report that they often do, and more strongly in men than women, spend time making themselves look as feminine as they can, as well as in an androgynous style. They appear androgynous, the more likely they are to experience a more positive body image.

Crossdressing (CD) refers to men or women who, either occasionally or habitually, dress in clothes that are typically associated with individuals of the other biological sex and present their gender in order to emphasize physical gender dimorphisms, such that they can pass successfully as members of the other sex. This includes taking steps to hide biological signs of gender with things like breast forms or the use of facial makeup, as well as wearing/using clothes designed to exaggerate the form of the biological sex in which the individual is dressing. Whether or not these practices actually increase positive body image in this special study group of enhancement is yet to be objectively demonstrated and is the subject of the present study.

CHAPTER 11

Crossdressing and Relationships

Now I want to return to dress and relationships. My wife's initial enthusiasm when she encouraged me to crossdress diminished as she began to understand its meaning and significance for me. This is, unfortunately, an outcome reported by many of us in heterosexual relationships. After an initial period of acceptance, some wives move towards a position of 'tolerance', wherein they have few options besides accommodation and denial, and avoidance of any discussion of the topic. After ten years, my family reluctantly accommodated themselves to my dressing. They never interrogated me about it, and I never spoke to them about it until after detailing my feelings and aspirations in my 2002 essay. The essay was instrumental in initiating some sort of dialogue around an issue that had always been shielded from family or friends.

Male feminoles who frequent venues are in a position where they are not compelled to involve immediate others. Wearing attire typically reserved for women, and designing, transforming, and nurturing a female persona are often solitary practices. In part, male feminoles pursue this estranged trajectory because of the potential alienation and critical appraisal they might experience in society.

They practice femininity in a distant and controlled way through literature, the internet, and the construction of a site-of-woman. Relationships between male feminoles frequenting such venues are usually superficial and based upon appearance and mutual support. They are impersonal in the sense that they do not desire to truly extend themselves to a profound understanding of others' feminizing strategies. This pattern of interaction is paradoxical, although communal and transactional in the formation of a community-of-women, the events are devoid of any real intimacy between participants. This lack of intimacy is caused by the fact that they only display their femininity as some kind of commodity.

CHAPTER 12

Legal and Ethical Considerations

As well as the moral judgments imposed by society, there is a legal obligation to conform with the gender assigned to persons at birth. The right to self-definition through the available options of legal gender recognition is subject to known, regionally varying national norms, laws, and requirements. Some laws may oblige the person to live in the gender role that reflects their gender identity for a certain period of time or to be sterile (primarily, to have undergone gender affirmation surgeries that result in infertility) or physically altered in order to be issued with the necessary documents. It may place a duty on the person to publicize their transgender status by obtaining a medical health certificate or related evidence that may help to protect them under anti-discrimination laws, but may also undermine their right to privacy.

It is important for healthcare practitioners and crossdressers to be aware of legal obligations that potentially affect them, but that are not always determined by officially accessible laws and texts. Ethical considerations, rather than strict laws and regulations, may also influence individual rights and freedoms. Ethical considerations are also driven by deeper social norms about the essentialness of natural masculinity and femininity. Even when acting legally, crossing the boundaries of bodily gender presentation may result in negative reactions from individuals or groups. These reactions have been exacerbated by the publicity and moral panic related to gender issues as well as the fear of sexual predators gaining access to single-sex spaces for sexual crime. Determinations of where the acceptable practices of crossdressers and transgender persons should end and where the right to privacy and access to single-sex spaces should be upheld are lacking. Publicity about gender identity issues, while helping to solve some problems by raising society's awareness and recognition of transgender rights, can also lead to increased experiences of transphobic actions and violence.

CHAPTER 13

Crossdressing in the Workplace

Ethical Dilemma: Cross-dressing in the Workplace

Cross-dressing in the workplace serves to further underscore the difficulty of maintaining an overall sense of wholeness for some individuals. Shary Warner, for example, describes a number of particularly troubling issues that male crossdressers face when trying to come to terms with their own identities—accepting themselves as crossdressers. For some, fantasy life provides a way to do so in private. Others wish to make cross-dressing a more public and integrated part of their identity and generally speaking, there is little option to do so while still meeting the expectations of society. Certainly, the expected gender-attributed roles of women are not the same as those for men; the two sets of roles are relatively incompatible. As Legman wrote, "To most women, femininity is a business, a way to get a man, to keep a man, and to hang onto the security represented by the man." It is due to the workplace that many extreme efforts have been made to carry out lifelong transformations from male to female. In the main, the situations in the workplace often reflect the values of the dominant white, male, middle-class culture, and it is often to this that groups use as benchmarks and perceived as "the way it should be." Because of this situation, many men and women also perceive the workplace as a dangerous place where detection would have an impact on their social status and self-image. Detection could mean the end of a goal, not because of the activities but because of the stigma created by the mainstream stereotypes. Moreover, job security, pay, or promotions could also be an issue.

Here is a tale in point that illustrates the lifestyle changes adults prepare for preoperative and for the gender numbers of businesses who wish to accommodate and include such individuals. Clara is a 40-year-old male-to-female postoperative housewife. Up until a year ago, she was an electronics engineer with a local computer company. (It is necessary to understand a two-year period between when Clara began male feminization in another city, a system initiated by another agency, which had a medical team that included psychiatrists and psychologists, two physical endocrinologists, cosmetic surgeons, and a cultural therapist, and the time she began the job search and the development of an employer/employee relationship with the computer company.) Prior to that, Clara had been hesitant about entering the workforce as a woman. She worried that people would connote her work performance or capacity to work with her male-to-female transsexual status. She decided, however, that arranging an interview as a man could also be a potential problem. She thus feminized into a "pretty man" and described herself to the potential employer as "a transvestite (diagnosed) with a potential worldview dangerousness to the skeleton of the computer world." Later, after working for the company for a bit over a year, Clara told the personnel managers the truth, and the team and medical team again, to avoid any potential problems of fear of loss of job or of future free employment. (Her father, whom she described, could go to the "briny bottom" of hell for support, had provided her with attorney contact information before her disclosure.) Clara's immediate reaction was "Thank God, we have been prepared and in still, I panicked and have been tense for days, but basically, I did not want to be paying for security, or fearing the unknown." Rather than scurry, the company employed her through the transitional period and became a major supporter, agreeing to allow her part-time flexibility; she now focuses her efforts on domestic matters and charity organizations in Little Rock. This is interesting because I believe the parallel lifestyles, and the similarity, suggest a way to develop service.

CHAPTER 14

Crossdressing and Fashion

The idea of using fashion to express oneself may also be applied to the study of crossdressers. One of the few studies exploring the way in which crossdressers use fashion is that of Leng (2002), who interviewed Japanese "new half" and "half" crossdressers. She suggested that the new half crossdressers, often called "shemale" in Thailand, and the half crossdressers negotiate their femininity, masculinity, and fashion through the use of different elements of the fashion system. I want to take this idea of crossdresser fashion a little further and use this understanding to explore the wider workings of the practice of crossdressing, which consists of more than just adopting the clothing of the opposite sex.

There are a number of reasons why men might adopt a female appearance. For some, changing their clothing is the first move toward complete sex change operations. Indeed, transvestism and transsexualism are often confused in everyday language. The terms themselves overlap, with many transvestite support groups also sharing space with transsexual support groups. Also, crossdressing and then sex reassignment is an established point of transition in the new Danish sex-change operation program (Bullit, 1970). However, many drag queens, female impersonators, and transvestites have no desire for or have given up on the idea of sex reassignment. Then, of course, there are those who do it simply for pleasure. Crossdressing may be a form of private kink or done more publicly as a form of entertainment. It is a fascination with the bricolage of classical femininity and where the male body "turns" female. For them, crossdressing is simply recreating the difference between woman and man.

CHAPTER 15

Crossdressing and Performance Art

Crossdressing is often discussed through or in relation to art, and quite certainly, crossdressing can be a powerful and effective art form. Indeed, it is often combined with performance or other art forms to make a powerful critique of art as an institution, art history, contemporary society, and/or the combination of these. It used to be nearly the only alternative for trans* people who wanted to gain some kind of existence, recognition, or be public (in some societies/countries, this is what crossdressing still is). And last but not least (for this never will end), crossdressing is also very much related to sexual performances and to drag, to the many ways one can express one's own identity – whether this means to hide or to reveal one's own identity.

There is also a vast and exciting tradition of women crossdressing to be on stage in men's roles, in various European, Asian, and other theatre traditions. In Brecht's 'Mutter Courage', the protagonist is also male-performed in many productions, even if also female-performed. The wide range of meaning and expression of these feminizations – from humiliation and punishment of the victim in various ways to a source of strength and self-identification – only goes to show that any layering of identity and power can be at work with male performance of femininity. Male feminization presents a whole other set of questions and meanings than performance art, for sure.

CHAPTER 16

Crossdressing and Technology

The development of the internet and global digitalization has enabled people to connect worldwide, discuss their practices, share experiences, and read personal accounts from other cross-dressers. Online forums and groups like crossdressers.com, Reddit AMAs, or Susans.org have provided space for voices and visibility and easily enable information exchange and support from and for people new to the world of crossdressing. However, the ease of access and exchange has also led to an increased supply of information and commercial offers (e.g. wigs, clothing, breast forms) or counseling to "cure" cross-dressers. People who have observed a feminization trend also struggle with increased popularization and commercialization, fearing that the "solutions" might lead to further defining the interest as a mere fetish.

People who are unable or unwilling to present female in public are grateful that they still have the option to "virtually" pass as a female either in private live sessions on the internet or through virtual character creations such as the games The Sims or Second Life. In such online games, people are able to (re)create an identity as slender Caucasian girls if they want to, but in non-utopian whiteness black people, racism, and othering are still taking place and social hierarchies can still be reproduced. The creation of female characters in games, also known as "genderbending" in the literature, is usually primarily male.

CHAPTER 17

Crossdressing and Online Communities

Crossdressing has, for many people, been a predominantly solitary practice conducted away from the view of others. Online communities have, however, created unprecedented potential for crossdressers to reach one another. In displaying their crossdressing to supportive communities, men can gain affirmation for a self they feel is intrinsically part of them; they get to step out of invisibility. Many have found consolation in acquiring a term for their behavior and corresponding self-perception, perhaps have started to regard the colorful stigma as a potentially positive stereotypic marker. Indeed, just as the concept of 'crossdressing' has offered a sense of self-affirmation for some transvestites, the concept of crossdresser has done the same.

With this entire spectrum of gender drag, various idols – masculine, feminine, androgynous, and gynandrous – tout and celebrate a form of glamour that is true to the crossdressers' inner self. John arranges online drag make-over evenings through 'Sarah's super site'. A number of chat rooms on the 'Be-all' website facilitate the live running of a 'make-over chat room, and only women may give input.' He intends to arrange a 'Makeover, Tips, and Pictures' section on his own webpage and is also considering posting stories by 'other individuals' in Team 'Girls Night In'. There seems to be 'only room for nice people'. Within this virtual room, masculinity is deconstructed. In meetings such as 'Sarah's', women help men become more feminine using, in this case, wigs and makeup. There is a curious dialectic inhering in the recursion of these spaces. On one hand, the men within the heterosexual drag use women to suggest feminine identities of themselves that are indications of their own inner selves and thereby feminize them, at least metaphorically and temporally.

CHAPTER 18

Crossdressing in Non-Western Cultures

Crossdressing in non-Western cultures also offers compelling insights into the meaning and practices of crossdressing, both in general and more specifically when undertaken by or on behalf of males. Tschandala's article on crossdressing among Cambodian men explores "an order of appearance" and a representation of the body that is heavily mediated through the fetish image and the pornography that creates the fetish image. In these sites, the image of the male body as primary becomes not only strained but also over-determined and irrelevant. When cross-dressed males are considered beautiful, it is a kind of beauty that is typically reserved for fetishized or marginalized populations. This aesthetic constitutes a complex and mixed signal. On the one hand, it is a signal of how people can be permanently reduced to their surface appearance and how that appearance can be over-determined by the meanings invested in visual representations that visualize phobic narratives of existential diminution, obduracy, and overvalued immanence. On the other hand, such an aesthetic could be a visual recuperation of these very decadent slave meanings, as the process of over-determination can have complex effects on the meaning of embodiment.

This transvestite (tseuttae) is often derided as a wild character, a fool who always wants food and jokes as well. He may go out alone when he has a craving for a saucy song or dance. He accosts young men, lures them to him for a chat, and may haunt them in lonely places. Some scuttle off as fast as they can, but others are drawn to him and gaily chat. Finally, "If I could be one of your sweeties, your beauty makes my heart throb, and to have the joy of being loved by you would be enough to pull a cow out of the mudhooke," he will say, and the youth flattered will laugh with delight at this old, old jest flung at him.

CHAPTER 19

Crossdressing in Religion and Spirituality

The religious and spiritual implications of the act of crossdressing are, in their own right, a complex and highly contextual matter. In a pre-Christian Celtic society, a battagie or Votay usually played one of various roles, among them the priest, but he lived and dressed in women's clothes throughout the year. However, it was known in Christianized Scottish Highlands that a woman dressed as a man could work as a preacher, teacher, or bridge toll keeper. Ireland even had a ritual with a man dressing as a woman. Some tales end in eventually learning the incumbent's true nature and stripping him of his ability to act as the religious authority. This perception that witches dressed as men and men dressed as women was a belief possibly due to the fear and fascination by society upon those who step outside of the conventional gender binary, possibly as an overall power trip, a desire for transcendence, or disruption of the status quo by women who have little agency of societal change. In some works of fiction, however, the andrógina or Híbalo are seen as the strongest characters because they break all rules set according to gender.

A paper entitled "Righteous Men Who Engaged in Martial Cross-Dressing" researched contemporary records of two Jews in Christian-dominated lands. They were one Saadia ben Eleazar ben Saadia and Meir ben Eleazar, both known as the 'man-dressed woman who arose in the congregation' or the 'wicked man called the man-dressed woman who arose in the congregation'.

It was reported by three witnesses. One was a fisherman known as Xomus de Trini, who said he saw Saadia being stripped to the waist so that he could be flogged. Saadia attempted to climb onto the scaffold but was prevented by a man named Servane. Saadia was imprisoned along with some of his judicial co-sharers in the former court of law of Audiencias of new criminal law-matters. Saadia was later fished from the waters. Saadia was tortured in his own words "like a woman" and "beaten and tortured as befitting one in raiments of feminine attire". "The one stripped sought to raise his or her chest in an unnatural manner" and "When the bailiffs bound him, he laughed"; while being raised he said to the audience "keep that crime, which has so heavily burdened me, concealed completely from your memory with a covering of charity." Saadia continued to say that the Inquisitor should check him for heresy "He would realize that my belief is pure like fallen dew and that I sin under the compulsion of wicked people". This paper provides a small window on Jews who dressed in clothes of the neither/nor.

CHAPTER 20

Crossdressing and Self-Expression

It was through the lens of self-fashioning that the exploration of crossdressing as a form of self-mediated representation emerged as the core of my study. I wanted to discern the characteristics that distinguish men's crossdressing from their wardrobe choices, and I learned that the language of explanation for audible events mirrored the goals and beliefs promoted through crossdressing as an action. As one would assume, crossdressers themselves view crossdressing as a unique form of expression through which they communicate many aspects of themselves, including their social selves, emotions, female self-perceptions, and what I call the crossdressing-enantio-dromia experience. The social and often complex network of self-expression motivations for use of transvestism as were revealed in my work can often only be conveyed through the act of getting dressed, a process Nancy Kelley describes in "The Long Time Ago Article". Only when fully dressed may a crossdresser "look in the mirror and see a reflection of oneself. I don't mean just the clothing and what makeup my sister put on me, but the way I look."

In research done by psychologists Paul A. Fedoroff, A. Jamie Cutler, and Ray A. Bradford, the concept of true self-emergent self was described in greater detail. It was found that crossdressing is often endowed with a "distinct psychoemotional significance" inasmuch as it becomes an "enacted self" through a special, separate ritual. I posited that Erik Erikson's model of self-identity, as discussed in "Childhood and Society", was a helpful tool for understanding how Eriksonian theories could be applied to my data and furthered the conceptualization of crossdressers as active agents. Erikson argued that the nature of a people's play reflects their self-identity. At each stage, the child's play activities teach him about the immediate world and, in turn, about himself. Children act out times they feel creative, times that they refuse to compromise their true selves.

CHAPTER 21

Challenges and Stigma Associated with Crossdressin

My interest and fieldwork in crossdressing have led me to discover that for many people, crossdressing is an experience that is often deeply engulfed. It proved to be exceedingly difficult for my conversations to maintain the informants' anonymity, and not because of the oddness of the jacket and glasses. Informants are suspended and immobilized between the possibility of being seen or "outed" and a protective, hypervigilant isolation. In keeping with my informants, the basis for crossdressing should be imperative and as long as it does not harm others. Still, the mere possibility of being seen as a man in a skirt, for example, can produce intense anxiety and apprehension, as well as a struggle to deflect and reassure yourself among the impact.

She told me he had to inform his future partner after the penalty and worried about being judged and asked how he kept the information away from her. I replied with one of the stories he had told: I explained to her, and her anxieties evaporated, that some were cruel, and some left. She replied that it must work like some of the therapy practices we use; otherwise, how could she go further with me?

In the last five years, I have received similar responses to my work from clinicians and trans researchers. These responses indicate to me a growing rift in how we think about alleging a "true" trans identity. Authentically, the "preferred" languages of selfhood, permitting no gray territory, no in-between, and asserting their voices overwhelmingly characterize the two differing traditions.

CHAPTER 22

Support and Resources for Crossdressers

There are a number of ways for crossdressers to develop an improved self-concept. Some individuals seeking improvement in self-identity pursue cross-dressing as a means for self-expression, and others report that they cross-dress to resolve internal conflict with their gender identity. Either way, seeking support and resources for such individuals are a critical component of counseling. Crossdressers who are seeking to resolve conflict with their gender identity often feel very isolated. They often do not know about other people who deal with the same issues and believe that their behavior is considered deviant or immoral by others in their religious group, their family, or their friends. The SOFFA often knows the pathway to community organizations that can provide support and corroborate the crossdresser's belief in self-acceptance.

One of the organizations that has established several chapters throughout the US and could advocate for group cohesiveness and interior acceptance is the Tri-Ess Society for the Second Self. Tri-Ess and associated chapters are a support/social organization for heterosexual crossdressers and their families. The Tri-Ess chapters sponsor spouses and significant others in Friends of Tri-Ess and their children in a group called Chi Rho Family. Tri-Ess' educational mission is to get on talk and news programs to educate the public about crossdressers and develop a support network for crossdressers. In this important time frame—the early years of interactions with similar others—crossdressers need the compassion of SOs and a social work counselor or consultant who can direct them to a well-established framework of acceptance as they deal with new feelings and savor the joy of acceptance that they have longed for. More worldly counselors, some clergy, and some clinics sponsor support groups specifically for crossdressers around the country.

CHAPTER 23

Research Methods in Studying Crossdressing

This review seeks to explore identity fluidity through an analysis of crossdressing (the wearing of clothing typically associated with another gender), finding that crossdressing describes a way in which some people can explore and come to understand some aspects of their identities as open, flexible, and fluid, never reducible to biological sex. The authors are especially interested in "male feminization," which here is simply a way of one person exploring what feminization would look and feel like on their own body, without any direct connection to sex work. We would also like to focus on the independent, migrant individuals who crossdress and feminize as a part of casually exploring how they might experience their gender and bodies. Our fifth, and final, interest in the concept of crossdressing is where it might lead: hopeful of and inspired by the potential of these practices as a way to (re)orient self to body, we are in the process of developing an application using photo manipulation for those who are interested in exploring or getting a "sneak peek" at what their feminized selves might look like.

Interdisciplinary approaches to exploring these resources and practices may begin with the more historical script. This research project adopts an approach to our participants' lived experiences that acknowledges the complex ways in which sexuality and gender are enacted, performed, and/or embodied in everyday life. Developing our study with reference to earlier work in which male cross-dressers and transvestites were found to employ resources that included culturally received discursive script and specific embodied practices, we decided to carry out detailed observations of our participants' appearances in order to identify whether there exist recognizable identifiable elements of the same or a similar script of feminization. The aim here was to be involved in elaborating a broader background for the ongoing discussions of the various ways in which people carry out practices of feminization and/or cross-dressing. Gathering such data required that we make visible and openly offer our participation in the spectacle of feminization. The following review details the methods we used and the ethical considerations for collecting data for our research.

CHAPTER 24

Conclusion and Future Directions

This book has provided some insights into crossdressing and female/feminine genders, the practice of male feminization, and men attracted to feminized men. In doing so, there are some directions that now present themselves for future research. It would be very beneficial to design formal research to assess how elements taken from drag and used in the process of feminizing men resonate with crossdressers and their experiences. A more general study with greater numbers would provide a starting place in terms of reporting the practice or interest in male feminization and the motives for this drive, as well as men's experiences with this sex/gender genre.

More nuanced study could enable an exploration into whether male feminization is more of an interest to crossdressers who are attracted to other men and it would be comprehensible and desirable to consider the value of exploring the backgrounds of crossdressers in more detail, such as liquor, class, sexuality and what might seed the desire to cross powerfully enough as to surmount barriers particularly as crossdressers in training. Indeed, it raises questions around physical representation, body-concordant surgeries, and the nurturing of an ERT/anti-androgen technique – even amongst the minority of crossdressers who are ERT-undertaking men in South Korea, hormone names and methods differ. It also rings alarm bells for medical practitioners. This research and commentary calls for questioning – what, exactly, do people wish for, in respect to their bodies and identities, and why? And, in choosing to help people towards ideal goals, psychiatry must not direct as much as accompany and investigate, the self-creations of those it attends. What remains here may be a considered response to suffering – aiding, through evidence, literature and empathy, the creation of worlds worth living.